HOW TO
BONK
IN PUBLIC

Authors' dedication

To Hugh Grant, who doubtless regrets that this book was not published earlier…

WARNING

WELBECK PUBLISHING DENIES RESPONSIBILITY FOR ANY PROBLEMS YOU MAY ENCOUNTER BY BONKING OUTDOORS AND FOR ANY OTHER PROBLEMS YOU MAY FACE BY FOLLOWING ANY OF THE JOKEY ADVICE IN THIS HUMOROUS BOOK. WE ARE NOT RESPONSIBLE.*

Published in 2021 by Welbeck
An Imprint of Welbeck Non-Fiction Limited,
part of Welbeck Publishing Group
20 Mortimer Street, London, W1T 3JW

Text copyright © 2021 Mats and Enzo
Design copyright © 2021 Welbeck Non-Fiction Limited,
part of Welbeck Publishing Group

First published by Prion Books in 2011

A CIP catalogue record for this book is available from the British Library

ISBN 978-1-78739-819-1

Printed in Spain

10 9 8 7 6 5 4 3 2 1

* But we will be proud of you!

HOW TO BONK IN PUBLIC

A handy guide to getting the best
sex in all sorts of places, from the
ski slopes to the supermarket

Mats & Enzo

WELBECK

CONTENTS

Would you like to have more sex?
Then this is the book for you!

You have read dozens of versions of the *Kama Sutra*, memorized them and tried all the positions. The reverse Lotus? You've done it in your kitchen, on the washing machine, on the couch, on your rug, on the floor, in the bathroom, on the sink, in the hallway, on the stairs… Same goes for the Windmill, the Wheelbarrow, the Frog and pretty much all other positions from the *Kama Sutra*. Fortunately, you had the good fortune of getting hold of this book. It will help you discover all the new possibilities that sex in public can bring.

There are some surprises in store, and we will reveal several sexual positions that have never been seen before.

The book is based on the findings of the biggest study ever done on the subject of public bonking, numerous testimonials and much field work: for over a year, we have done it as many times as we could, sometimes up to 12 times a day, in all weather conditions and in all types of places. As in our other works (on the subjects of pooing at work, bonking at work and pooing on holiday), we drew up another reference book and we are especially proud of its content (our families aren't, however). But just like you, researchers and university professors across the globe have been waiting impatiently for this book to deepen their theoretical knowledge. And since we firmly believe that being able to bonk in public is a basic human right, we wanted this book to be sold at an affordable price. Those who just look at it and smile rather than try out some of the solutions it suggests will be worse off, but incredible sensations are in store for everyone else.

Bonk in public to reach higher in your life!

BONKING IN PUBLIC: AN EFFICIENT SOLUTION FOR ONE-NIGHT STANDS

The one-night stand is a pleasant and playful activity. However, everyone who practices it inevitably faces problems. In fact, just seconds after kissing your conquest, problems begin: how can I get him/her back to my place? Saying "Come on, let's go back to my place so I can give you one" does not lead to fruitful results. A more effective solution – strategy if you will – is needed.

The most frequent technique consists of using sentences like "Do you want to come back to my place for a nightcap?" Or "Would you come back to my place so I can show you my green toaster?" And so on until the partner says yes.

When such a proposal works, nothing has yet been gained. The question of transportation to your domicile lingers. It can be difficult to maintain the sexual tension between the two of you during this time. For example, if going to your place requires a two-hour bus and underground ride or an hour in the back of a Renault 5, the sexual tension is sure to drop.

Those partaking in one-night stands (ONS) are no strangers to the fact that problems also arise the next morning: the bad surprise of a partner who in the daylight turns out to be unpleasantly fat is quite common. However, if instead of taking your conquest home you chose to bonk in public, you would be left with that good (alcohol-induced) impression of the person the next day. There would also be no bad breath situation, or an endless breakfast where you realize you have nothing to talk about, and no problem of the partner who makes themselves at home at your place and just won't leave.

It is quite clear that bonking in public is a very effective solution to such problems. You will no longer have to lose time bringing your conquest back to your place; you will shag where you are, be it in a café, cinema, park or in the street.

By bonking at the site of your encounter, you will turn your one-night stands into ten-minute stands.

Take heed of the advice in this book and maximize your pleasure by ridding yourself of any and all ONS-related complications.

THE EXPERT: DICK JOHNSON

Dick Johnson has had a colourful life. Born to a family of several generations of construction workers, he got the idea for his future vocation while watching his father beating the ground with a jackhammer. He decided he did not want to waste his life with hard physical labour, and at a very young age had a brilliant idea: he decided to go into pornography. At 16 he began to practice for his future career in his room with the help of several inflatable dolls that he bought with his pocket money. He also put the family video camera to good use for this practice – something he had to stop rather abruptly when his entire family stumbled upon one of his productions as they all gathered to watch a video of the annual family vacation. When he was 18 and one day, he signed his first contract with a small production company and became the youngest male pornographic actor of all time.

It took him only three years to become hugely famous, thanks to his audacious outdoor sex techniques. On a hovercraft on the Thames, on the back of an elephant in India and even suspended from a helicopter over New York City: his fearlessness earned him a reputation as the leading porn actor of the 70s. All the producers were fighting to have him in their films, not only for his art and acrobatic talents, but also for his inimitable style: in the opening scenes of his films Dick always appeared in the same outfit: beige leather trousers and deep red velvet kangaroo briefs that went up to his navel. With that he wore his famous orange leather vest, skin-tight and low-cut so that his hairy chest was nicely visible. Today he is one of the last remaining representatives of the "hairy porn" era, the golden age of porn now long gone, when the actors also smoked during scenes. Dozens of Facebook groups are now asking for the return of hairy porn.

In a sad development for Dick, the mainstream porn industry went in a radically different direction. He refused to be a slave to the latest trends and declined to wax his torso and pubic hair, and still turns almost violent when someone suggests he wax his back. He could not see himself in this new era of porn, lacking elegance, so he made his exit, which understandably caused quite a stir among the remaining hairy porn fans.

This caused many to write him off, but they didn't count on his incredible capacity to come again. At 45 he went back to school, had much plastic surgery and gave up his velvet briefs for a three-piece tailored suit. He became an investment banker in New York with over a hundred clients. His great capacity for adaptation is now studied in all business schools.

But the very essence of a man cannot be changed. Dick Johnson remains a passionate man and has sex at least twice a day every day, no matter where he is (work, holiday, business trip) and no matter what company he is in.

We are grateful to our editor RH for introducing us to Dick and for being able to persuade him — no doubt thanks to their longstanding friendship (apparently they go back a long way together) — to serve as our expert in this book. Many thanks to Dick for sharing his experience so generously with us, thus helping us make this book even better.

Dick in 1976

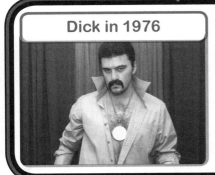

Dick in 2011

BONKING IN NATURE
– THE ORIGIN OF THE SPECIES.

An anthropologist tells us all about the sexual encounters of prehistoric people

100,000 years ago, people's principal activity was shagging outdoors; much more so than hunting or smearing coloured mud the walls of caves. (That is why your book is so much more fascinating in fact). It is thanks to thousands of such sex games the human species has survived. We are all, in fact, proud descendants of these outdoor bonking people.

Formerly, the seduction process nothing like it is nowadays; oh no... The man dragged the woman around by her hair to show that he was interested. The woman then performed a little erotic show by gently hitting herself with small tree branches to indicate her agreement. To make things easier, certain males knocked females out before the act. (We believe that this practice has led to the "starfish" position that many women still adopt today when having intercourse with men who are only interested in their own pleasure.) Other men, however, were already showing signs of romance by building cosy beds made of twigs outside their dwellings. The women that the men didn't find sufficiently hairy were not chosen (the hairiness of men and women was significant at the time, and brushing tools did not exist).

In the evening, sex was practiced next to the fire, which explains our remaining affinity for romantic evenings by the fireplace or over candles. Some bonked by the fire while others sharpened their tools and discussed the next hunt. In time some of them, tired of spending entire evenings polishing pieces of rock, started to comment on the frolics of those next to them and giving advice such as: "I wouldn't do it that way." Or: "Go behind her, you will see better." And: "Do you want me to help you lift her up? And even: "What, you are finished already?" Sometimes they even tried to join in with those having sex. To avoid such situations, couples started to move towards the caves and grottos in order to bonk in peace.

This is how the practice of having sex indoors began and remained common to this day.

Having sex indoors was quite strange for people at first, and I believe that a book entitled *How to Bonk Indoors* would have sold very well indeed at the time.

This major sociological evolution has made us the indoor sexual beings that we are today. It has also progressively led to the almost complete loss of hair, since the need to stay warm when bonking outside has gone. Women began to improve the caves – the bonk space – and make them more comfortable; they also developed an interest in interior decoration. As for the men, they started to draw the sexual orgies of their forefathers on the walls of the caves as a way of passing on the cultural heritage.

Today, none of the cave paintings of the outdoor sex period remains. Those who discovered such paintings in the early 20th century were very much under the influence of the puritanical values of the day, and covered up thousands of ancient paintings depicting sexual orgies which the ancient Romans and today's porn actors would surely be envious. Aware of the cultural shock such discovery would cause if made public, they jointly decided to cover these paintings completely and in their place drew ridiculous simple scenes of prehistoric man chasing wild horses or bears.

In conclusion, I would like to add that it was only much later, when man began cultivating land instead of hunting, that the second sexual revolution occurred. Man worked the land during the day and scheduled indoor sex for the evening. It is this much less amusing and much more limiting model that is unfortunately in place still today.

Fred Smith, Anthropologist

PART 1:

PLACES AND POSITIONS
- THE OUTDOOR BONKASUTRA

Our expert has selected 54 positions to help you discover a magical world where imagination, enthusiasm, trees and sensuality meet.

Where to bonk?

How do you know for sure that a position you are considering is well adapted to the place where you are bonking?

How do you help your partner discover positions that are completely new to them?

In the following pages you will discover that it is even possible to bonk in your supermarket trolley, among other places...

BONKING AT THE BEACH

Ideal for: All-night bonk/Romantic bonk/Coco Bonk
Arousal level: 3/5
Probability of being caught: 5/5 during the day; 1/5 during the night
Possibility of finding additional partners: 5/5 during the day;
3/5 during the night

PLUSES & MINUSES

+ Possibility of including your inflatable crocodile in your frolicking and doing a beach threesome.
+ During a night bonk the darkness will help you forget that your partner is not exactly sexy; in fact that they are downright ugly.
+ Free back scrub for whoever is underneath.

- You risk being attacked by a seagull.
- A dog may run up to you and sniff your intimate areas.
- A crab pinch in an unfortunate spot is always painful.

When to go

At night.

Expert's opinion

When you are at the beach at sunset during your next holiday, be aware that all those people walking up and down hand in hand aren't there just for a stroll. They are all looking for a bonk spot, and they are all in each other's way. *Result:* nobody bonks.

The happy grotto

Expert's opinion

Whoever is on the back should hold the handles tightly. Otherwise the first gust of wind will have you running naked around the beach trying hopelessly to catch the inflatable boat that will be flying farther and farther from your reach.

The great baywatch

lifeguard

Expert's opinion

In the off-season I come to the beach with swimming shorts and a red buoy that I bought at www.becomemitchbuchannon.com. I pretend to be a lifeguard. When I first tried this I was dubious it would actually work, but I was surprised to see how successful it was: with the help of my red buoy I bonked at least six times a day in the lifeguard hut.

The scented control tower

Expert's opinion

If you fancy a citronella-scented sauna before or after bonking, go into the port-a-loo (it has been out in the scorching sun the whole day).

A cone with two scoops

Expert's opinion

I recently tried the cone with two scoops position. In the excitement I did not notice that one of my feet got stuck inside the ice cream tub. It was impossible to get it out and I had to walk with my foot stuck in the tub all the way back to my place.

The enchanted coconut

Expert's opinion

Make sure you don't shake the tree too much — being hit by a fallen coconut is very, very painful.

The bonk-brella

Expert's opinion

If somebody comes out of the hut to complain about the drumming noise, tell them that you are teaching your partner how to do a handstand.

BONKING AT THE CINEMA

Ideal for: A quick bonk/3D surround bonk
Arousal level: 4/5
Probability of being caught: 3/5
Possibility of finding additional partners: 1/5 *
(* some people actually turn up to watch films)

PLUSES & MINUSES

+ One of the few places where it's dark all the time.
+ If your partner is ugly, you can look at the screen and imagine you are bonking with the actress or actor in the film.
+ Everybody bonks at home before going to sleep. But we forget that bonking at the cinema saves us a precious hour of sleep.

- If your neighbours see what you're doing they will be more interested in your actions than in the film.
- Considering the ever-rising cost of movie ticket prices it is becoming uneconomical to not watch the film.
- If you bonk in the aisle you risk tripping up people who are going to the toilet during the film.

When to go

During the showing, otherwise see under "Bonking in the parking lot."

Expert's opinion

Careful: if your partner smells funny, has an oddly long tongue and has a moustache, you are probably not kissing the right neighbour…

The carnal shadow

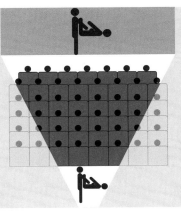

Expert's opinion

You should only do this in art-house cinemas, where the audience will think the shadows are part of the director's vision.

The Rodeo

Expert's opinion

If the person in front of you looks under the seat, simply smile and say "Hello!" without any explanations.

23

The wheelbarrow of the seventh art

Expert's opinion

If she gets very hungry during this, she can simply pick up some popcorn from the floor, or even better, from tub of the person sitting in front of you.

The head rest

Expert's opinion

Careful, if you're not in the last row you risk blocking the view of others.

The monkey man

Expert's opinion

For better balance, she can put her head in the cup holder.

The horny janitor

Expert's opinion

If someone asks what you are doing, just say that you are picking up the popcorn you dropped on the floor.

25

BONKING AT THE SWIMMING POOL

Ideal for: Aquabonk / Quick bonk / Weightless bonk
Arousal level: 3/5
Probability of being caught: 2/5
Possibility of finding additional partners: 3/5

PLUSES & MINUSES

+ Possibility of using your softboard as a soft-core spanking paddle.
+ Possibility to enact your eternal fantasy: bonking in a duck rubber ring, inflatable armbands and a latex bathing cap.
+ For the S&M lovers: if the lifeguard sees you, he may try to make you stop by hitting you with his pole.

- Bonking in a swimming pool is guaranteed to give you thrush or a badly placed wart.
- Certain swimming pools have glass walls that allow the patrons of the adjacent bar observe what is going on in the water.
- Serious risk of drowning when attempting the more complex positions of the *Kama Sutra*.

When to go

During the aquagym courses: take off your swimsuit, swim discreetly underwater towards the group and place yourself strategically under a participant.

Expert's opinion

Who hasn't seen couples kissing languidly at the edge of the swimming pool, not being able to go all the way because they haven't brought a condom?

The high doggy style

Expert's opinion

Gentlemen, if she is screaming very loudly this is not because you are giving her such pleasure but rather because she is afraid of heights.

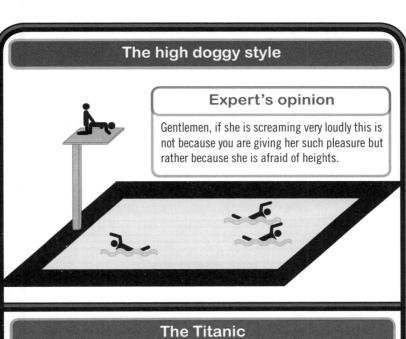

The Titanic

Expert's opinion

Each time I tried this position I found myself naked on the surface. It is impossible to stay on the bottom!

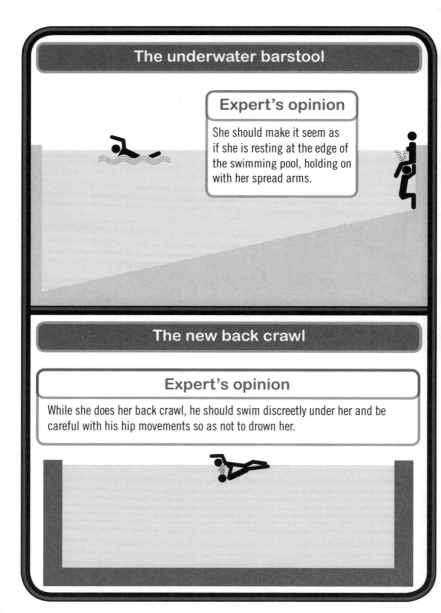

The underwater barstool

Expert's opinion

She should make it seem as if she is resting at the edge of the swimming pool, holding on with her spread arms.

The new back crawl

Expert's opinion

While she does her back crawl, he should swim discreetly under her and be careful with his hip movements so as not to drown her.

28

The Apneajob

Expert's opinion

To avoid floating up, the man should weigh himself down and the woman should hang on tight to his penis.

The magic body board

Expert's opinion

This position could lead to drowning.

BONKING ON A SKI TRIP

Ideal for: Slide bonk/Igloo bonk
Arousal level: 2/5
Probability of being caught: 2/5
Possibility of finding additional partners: 2/5

PLUSES & MINUSES

+ You are guaranteed to not break a sweat.
+ When it's very cold, you can create a first frozen sperm sample.
+ Possibility to do a group bonk in train formation on a bunny slope.

- The ski shoes make most of the *Kama Sutra* positions that are difficult to execute, and also represent a great danger for the gentlemen's "bits".
- It is challenging to turn on your partner when you are in a fluorescent ski suit and the protective lip balm gives your lips an eerie chalk-white shade.
- Positions requiring sitting can cause freezing of your bits. This is an awkward situation that can become even more embarrassing in a hospital emergency room.

When to go

When there's snow.

Expert's opinion

I recommend bonking every time you are in the cable car.

Snack break

Expert's opinion

Take a break during your descent: sneak behind the trees and bonk for a few minutes before continuing.

The enchanted dome

Expert's opinion

The igloos are often built by vacationers who may not be construction experts. Bonking while leaning on the igloo's walls can make you land in an Eskimo's living room...

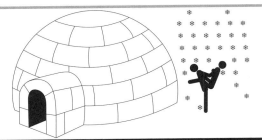

Porno toboggan

Expert's opinion

The glacial wind on your bits will bring you unforgettable sensations.

The blind passenger

Expert's opinion

When you go past the pillars she will think her partner is equipped with a natural vibrator.

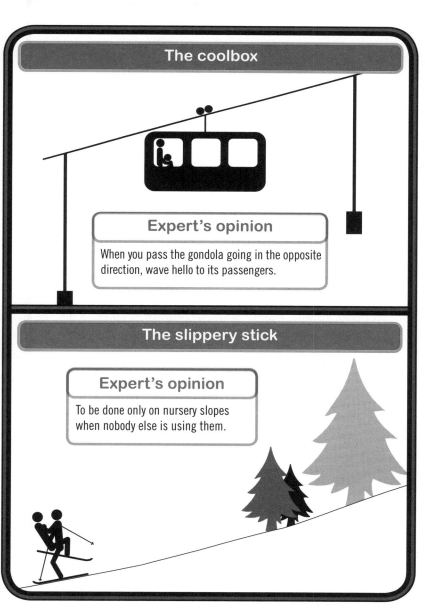

The coolbox

Expert's opinion

When you pass the gondola going in the opposite direction, wave hello to its passengers.

The slippery stick

Expert's opinion

To be done only on nursery slopes when nobody else is using them.

33

BONKING AT THE DISCO

Ideal for: Noisy bonk/Travolta-style bonk
Arousal level: 3/5
Probability of being caught: 1/5
Possibility of finding additional partners: 5/5

PLUSES & MINUSES

+ If your partner is ugly you can drink alcohol to stop caring.
+ Souvenir photos published the next day at www.disconightpics.net/'name_ of_your_disco.
+ If you are a fan of S&M there's a big chance that two huge bodyguards will rough you up and throw you out half naked if they find you bonking at the club.

- If you are not a fan of S&M: there's a big chance that two huge bodyguards will rough you up and throw you out half-naked if they find you bonking at the club.
- In the darkness we can easily confuse partners... and sadly it is rarely a good surprise once you see them in the daylight.
- While dancing happily by yourself, unwanted partners can rub against you in a way that suggests they would like to reproduce with you.

When to go

Before the cleaning staff cleans the very dirty place.

Expert's opinion

May I remind you that going to the disco with a partner is much like going to Frankfurt with a bunch of frankfurters – completely unnecessary. Be bold: go alone and try to bonk as much as possible.

The UBB: ultimate bass bonk

Expert's opinion

If a bodyguard arrives, tell him that you are holding her while she is looking for her keys.

The music box

Expert's opinion

Do any and all positions you want, as long as they don't require touching the walls or the toilet.

The wheelbarrow-colada

Expert's opinion

Here's a good activity to kill time while waiting for the barman to take your order.

The vibrating bed

Expert's opinion

No need for birth control in this position. The spermatozoa are being thrown about so violently with each bass beat that they lose their way. They are also under the influence of all the alcohol that you have had and are completely disoriented. They have no chance of making it to their destination.

The slow-blow

Expert's opinion

During your slow dance, go all the way with fellatio in the middle of the dance floor. Why do people so often go for half measures?

The drunken dog

Expert's opinion

If she is feeling ill, she will already be in the right position.

BONKING IN A THEME PARK

Ideal for: Bonk in disguise
Arousal level: 3/5
Probability of being caught: 4/5 during the day
Possibility of finding additional partners: 5/5

PLUSES & MINUSES

+ Possibility of doing a threesome with Asterix, a foursome with Mr & Mrs Ogre or a group bonk with the seven dwarfs.
+ Possibility of buying masks of some of the characters and bonking in disguise in a toilet restaurant. Very exciting.
+ You can turn on your partner during lunch by slowly licking a hotdog and looking at him/her intently.

- A blowjob on a rollercoaster can cause serious injury (both partners are concerned).
- Hearing "Hurry up, it's nearly time for the midday parade!" during conjugal activity in a public toilet can be very off-putting for a man.

Expert's opinion

I managed to get my hands on a study which found that 6.82% of visitors go to theme parks in the hope of getting rid of their kids for a few minutes to bonk in a hidden corner of the park. Many of the biggest parks have resisted creating porn franchises, despite my business plan that suggests billions could be made if one did.

Tea with spice

Expert's opinion

Due to the centrifugal force created by the rotation of the cups, blood will go to your brain faster and you risk "limp hose."

The wild rock

Expert's opinion

Don't be afraid of hurting your back – all the rocks in the park are made out of Styrofoam or cardboard.

Behind closed walls

Expert's opinion

A position that makes you feel like you are bonking in someone else's living room.

Masked up

Expert's opinion

Depending on your preferences, buy her a mask of your favourite character.

40

The fantastic ride

Expert's opinion

Opt for the back of the train and stay away from roller coasters that do too much looping.

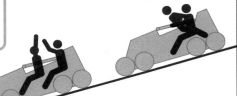

The choo-choo

Expert's opinion

Careful, if you are caught you will quickly have an audience bigger than that of the parade.

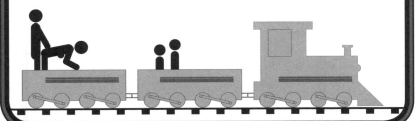

BONKING AT THE SUPERMARKET

Ideal for: Quick bonk/Vegetable bonk/Accessorized bonk
Arousal level: 3/5
Probability of being caught: 4/5 during the day
Possibility of finding additional partners: 3/5 during the day

PLUSES & MINUSES

+ You will find great material to make our best organic sex toys and use them right there and then.
+ Possibility of finding lots of cheap new underwear with your partner and trying it on five minutes later.
+ Possibility of rubbing your bodies with whipped cream or butter during the bonk.

- A frozen penis, which is a common result of bonking in a freezer, hidden under the frozen food.
- When we bonk at the supermarket we often come home without what we went there to get.
- Gentlemen, take care not to fall asleep under the fish counter afterwards.

When to go

Avoid weekends and family special events.

Expert's opinion

With some negotiating you could get a souvenir video from the supermarket security team.

The doggy cart

Expert's opinion

Feeling lazy? Place her on the trolley and push it back and forth.

The stockroom of ecstasy

Expert's opinion

If the forklift operator is on a break, I suggest you make the most of it by bonking in the forklift cab!

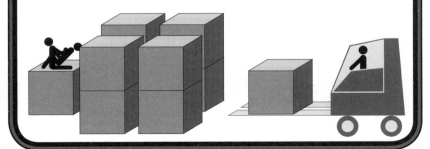

The banana pyramid

Expert's opinion

This reminds me of a scene in one of my first films, *The Fruit Orgy*. I was dressed as a banana and I had to bonk a big grapefruit and an apricot.

The contortionists

Expert's opinion

If one of you has bad breath, refreshing chewing gum is at an arm's length.

The short-sighted mole

Expert's opinion

Be careful not to confuse your partner with another customer. With their back turned towards you it is an easy mistake to make.

The magic trolley

Expert's opinion

Ask somebody to push you into the middle of the supermarket and yell: "I'm the king of the world!", like in *Titanic*.

BONKING IN A FURNITURE STORE

Ideal for: Quick Bonk/Ikea bonk/Accessorized bonk
Arousal level: 3/5
Probability of being caught: 4/5 during the day
Possibility of finding additional partners: 5/5 during the day

PLUSES & MINUSES

+ Possibility of properly testing your new bed.
+ If you stain anything there's no need to clean up; you can just leave.
+ Possibility of taking a quick shower before bonking.

- In 99% of cases, the showers in furniture stores don't work.
- Trying out 18 beds or more by bonking in them can become tiresome.
- If you break something you will have to pay for it.

When to go

Avoid if there's a sale on.

Expert's opinion

My observations suggest that over 90% of couples think of bonking when they are in furniture stores, but only 0.2% actually do it. And yet it is so easy to live out your fantasies in a cupboard, a bathroom, a kitchen... I myself bonk on all trips to furniture stores, whether I am with someone or not.

The classic

Expert's opinion

Careful, some beds are only there to look at and are not actually bolted together…

The blinding blowjob

Expert's opinion

Ladies, if the penis is cold, very hard and very long, you are probably licking a lamp.

The 3D

Expert's opinion

If a movie is on, other clients will be so blown away by the quality of the 3D that they won't even notice you bonking away next to it.

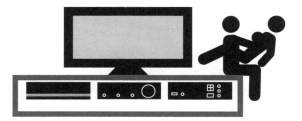

The magic box

Expert's opinion

Washing machine drums tend to have very good sound insulation. This is therefore a perfect position if she is a screamer.

The hot sofa

Expert's opinion

This is how I always choose a sofa, not like everybody else who just sits down.

The control tower

Expert's opinion

In a porno we would add a third actor on top of the cupboard. The girl would be giving him a blowjob simultaneously.

BONKING IN A PARK

Ideal for: Long bonk/Green bonk
Arousal level: 3/5
Probability of being caught: 4/5
Possibility of finding additional partners: 3/5

PLUSES & MINUSES

+ You can bonk in nature and not even leave the city.
+ No wild animals that could come and attempt reproduction with you.
+ Often there is a little stream where you can wash before or after.

- Even if there are no wild animals, a dog could come and sniff or lick you while you bonk.
- The hidden spots that are perfect for bonking are also the spots people use when they have to relieve themselves.
- Many curious old ladies, always looking for somebody to talk to.

When to go

Early in the morning, when joggers can become dynamic bonk partners.

Expert's opinion

Stop reading this book and go bonk in the nearest park immediately.

Banana and two olives skewer

Expert's opinion

I don't want to brag, but I was the first to manage this position, in the film *The Lumberjack's Big Chopper*.

Excited Tarzan

Expert's opinion

Ah, memories… This position was in the film *Another Portion of the Lumberjack's Big Chopper*.

The expandable bench

Expert's opinion

You should be (doubly) hard as a stick.

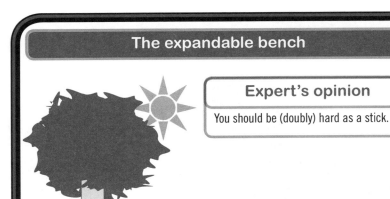

A basket with holes

Expert's opinion

Make her grab the dustbin firmly and go at it all the way!

PART 2:

Clearly, bonking outdoors is much more exciting than
a quickie at home after an evening of bad TV,
but it requires favourable conditions concerning
both the environment and your partner.

Problems Before

How do you get things started when your partner isn't as enthusiastic as you? What do you do if it's too cold and your equipment is freezing? How will you deal with odours you emit because you can't take a shower beforehand?

In the following pages you will find that it is possible to have a fantastic outdoor bonk, even if it doesn't last more than 37 seconds.

The situation

You are about to bonk outdoors. But there is a problem: it's winter and it's cold, so your tool gets teeny tiny. It's impossible to make it rise to the occasion.

The solution: The Swedish bath

1. Go into the nearest bar.
2. Order a hot chocolate.
3. Settle at a table.
4. Unbutton your trousers.
5. Place your equipment into the hot chocolate (just like when you dunk a donut into your coffee in the morning).
6. Keep this position until your equipment gets warm and properly dilated. This is a simple and well-known culinary technique, the *bain-marie*.
7. Leave the bar and commence as soon as possible with the bonk so that your penis doesn't turn into a chocolate popsicle.

Expert's opinion

Beware of another technique commonly used in such situations: the warming lighter. It tends to lead to the odour of grilled pork or even a pubic fire.

Testimonial

In these situations I like to go to a fast food stand and buy a fresh hotdog. I then switch the sausages.
Ben, 28

The situation

You develop the tendency of finishing too quickly. Since the idea of bonking outside excites you greatly, you tend not to last more than 37 seconds...

The solution: Kant

1. Avoid foreplay – you risk popping the cork before the party begins.
2. Get into position with your partner.
3. As soon as you begin, start pondering the following question:
   "Is it our awareness of death that creates in us the need for religion?" while dividing 14,273.52 by 85.427.
4. If all goes well this should make you last three minutes, the established time limit after which nobody can reproach you of anything.

Answer: 167.08.

Expert's opinion

I have nothing to say on this issue, since I hold the world record of the longest outdoor bonk: 8 hours and 47 minutes.

Testimonial

I told her: "I think this will last 37 seconds at most." She laughed, thinking I had just made a good joke. 37 seconds later, she wasn't laughing anymore.
William, 36.

You are caught with a prostitute

The situation

You go to see prostitutes because they are experts in public bonking. After picking a prostitute of foreign origin – which you established after hearing her strong accent when she suggested: "I do you big blow job" – you walk towards a bush with her when you bump into your mother.

The solution: Leopard Boots

1. Don't panic — even though there's plenty reason to. Say calmly: "Oh hello mother, good thing we bumped into you; you can help us with your opinion."
2. Go on: "I was just shopping with my friend Ursula who is looking for an outfit for her job interview on Monday. She bought these red fishnet stockings, white boots with 25 cm-high heels, a leopard print skirt and this fake fur coat. I can't make her understand that it makes her look a bit overdressed — could you explain it to her?
3. Your mother will answer that, indeed, the outfit is a little… risqué for a job interview.
4. Turn towards the prostitute and tell her: "See, I told you, you look a bit much with these clothes."
5. Say goodbye to your mother.
6. Run away.

Expert's opinion

My Dutch friend would like to launch a low-cost prostitute service in Amsterdam's red-light district. You book on the internet. The further in advance you book, the cheaper it is. While you are making love to her, the girl speaks commercials and tries to sell you extras: energy drinks, perfume, lottery tickets… To minimize the costs, the prostitutes spend their time between clients doing the accounts, updating the website …

Testimonial

My mother thought it was my new girlfriend and insisted she came home with us. The prostitute did not have a tariff for "family dinner" and charged me by the hour. When my mother suggested dessert, I was at €800. Steve, 33

The situation

You are shopping in the city centre. Suddenly you are taken by a great desire to bonk in public. Unfortunately, your partner doesn't feel like it.

The solution: The Acting Lesson

Here is our expert's method to create irresistible attraction. You should follow these steps one by one:
1. Look your partner in the eyes and caress your torso.
2. Buy an ice cream and lick it slowly and sensually.
3. Groan each time your partner looks at you.
4. Whip yourself with whatever you can find (electric cable, banana, belt…)
5. If your partner resists all these erotic advances, masturbate in the nearest changing rooms. Make sure they're empty first.

Expert's opinion

In the beginning I dreamed that real life would be like porn films, where everybody would always be up for sex. But I realized that this would be hell. Everybody would shag you within minutes of meeting them (the postman, the cashier, your neighbour etc.)

Testimonial

We were in the frozen food aisle of Tesco and I tried to turn her on by licking a frozen lasagne. My tongue got stuck on it.
Paul, 46

The situation

You are outside and your partner is as hot as a jalapeño. You, however, do not feel like it at all.

The solution: The conversation stopper

1. Tell your partner: "I understand that you are horny, but I don't feel very well today."
2. Your super-motivated partner will keep pressing, hoping you will change your mind.
3. Tell them: "You know, I feel a little queasy."
4. If your partner still insists, tell them: "Come on, give me a break, I have terrible diarrhoea. There, happy now?"
5. Walk away gingerly, holding your stomach and grimacing all the way.

Expert's opinion

Me, I'm always up for it.

Testimonial

I usually tell my girlfriend that I have a headache. If she insists, I say that I also have my period. I don't see why it shouldn't work for me too.
David, 31

You can't take a shower

The situation

You have a habit of taking a shower before making love. This time, you are outdoors and you feel like it, but you stink and there's nowhere to wash.

The solution: The Lynx effect

1. Head towards the nearest grocery store.
2. Buy a six-pack of sparkling mineral water and an exotically-scented bubbly shower gel.
3. Go back to the bonk area and undress.
4. Shake the mineral water bottles, pour them over your body and soap yourself up vigorously.
5. Go at it as if you were shooting a shower gel commercial. Get really into it, bite your lip, groan and say: "Oh yes, it's lovely to wash with bubbly shower gel!"
6. Then use a low (for men) or high (for women) voice and invite your partner to join you in the shower.
7. Bonk.

Expert's opinion

For those who would like to find out more about this subject, I am selling a best-of DVD with the sexiest scenes of all Palmolive and Lynx TV commercials from 1982 to the present today.

Testimonial

There was a water fountain nearby, so I jumped in. My partner joined me and we shagged like gods next to the Greek statues. The people were looking at us and they shouted and applauded. Our bonk is now on YouTube and we had 4,246,000 hits from Japan alone! It's nuts.
Veronica, 27

You are locked outside in an S&M outfit

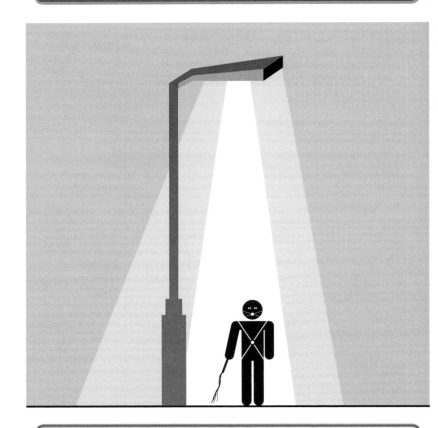

The situation

You put on your best S&M outfit: a tightly fitting latex body suit, head mask…
You step out for a second to get some air when a strong gust of wind slams
the door behind you and leaves you stranded outside.

The solution: The Venus de Milo

1. Head towards the nearest pedestrian area.
2. Find a solid cardboard box or a bottle crate.
3. Take off your mask and put it on the floor.
4. Climb on the crate and pretend to be a statue (like the fake marble statues seen performing in cities in the summer).
5. Don't move! If you are patient people will start to drop some money into your mask.
6. When you collect 100 euro, call a locksmith and go home.

NOTE: This is the last time that we can help you with such a stupid problem! We cannot always be there to help you with all the ridiculous situations you get yourself into. Next time take a minute to think before you walk outside in a black latex outfit!

Expert's opinion

If you also have chains, you can try to do a martial arts performance. This will make the money drop faster.

Testimonial

I live in a residential, family-oriented neighbourhood. I locked myself out in a blue and red latex suit. The neighbours' kids started shouting: "Daddy, come see! Our neighbour is dressed as Spiderman!"
Patrick, 42

PART 3:

Bonking outdoors can be full of surprises.

Unfortunately, many of them can prove to be... bad.

PROBLEMS DURING

What do you do if you are surprised during the act by a policeman who doesn't understand why you are naked in the middle of the street? How can you get rid of a wild animal that wants to play? What will you do when your partner has the awful idea of screaming "Ohhhh yess!" in the cinema?

In the following pages you will find that it is possible to come out unscarred when you are caught with your underwear round your ankles.

The situation

You are frolicking in the woods when a wild boar approaches — no doubt drawn by all the pheromones you are emitting. The boar looks very agitated.

The solution: The six-legged dragon

1. Stop your movements immediately.
2. Cover your intimate parts. The boar didn't come to observe you... he came to reproduce.
3. Face him.
4. Adopt the doggy-style position with your partner as fast as you can.
5. Shocked by this strange animal with two heads and six legs in front of him, he will run, horrified by the idea of becoming a sex toy for the sweaty dragon of the forest.

Expert's opinion

This reminds me of a Polish porn film from 1974. The main character wore a wild boar mask. The film bombed.

Testimonial

When I first saw the boar I thought he had five legs. It was only afterwards that I understood that he was just very, very excited.
Sophie, 32

You are bonking in your car and
are surprised by a policeman

The situation

You are fully in action in your car when a policeman knocks on the window.

The solution: The Scottish radiator

1. Tell the policeman: "Ah, officer, thank goodness you are here."
2. Continue: "We can't turn off the heating. The windows are completely foggy and with this heat, we had no choice but to take our clothes off."
3. Ask the policeman to help you: "With your experience, maybe you can tell us how we could turn down the heat?"
4. As soon as he touches a button – no matter which – thank and praise him: "Good job, officer, you are really very capable!"
5. Leave.

Expert's opinion

I read your other book, *How to Bonk at Work*. Like Steven Gooper I, too, got myself a shaggin' wagon. Mine is pink with a flashing light that comes on automatically when I'm bonking.

Testimonial

I was really aroused and I weighted up the situation badly. I said to him: "Oh officer, take out your club and hit me everywhere with it!"
Diego, 26

You have cramp

The situation

There's a draft where you are bonking and it gives you bad cramp. You know that it will leave you paralyzed in a painful and rather dubious position.

The solution: The Stretch

1. As soon as you start feeling the cramp, stop moving.
2. Tell your partner you have cramp (there will be disappointment, especially when they see that your shrieks weren't caused by pleasure, but rather intense pain).
3. Tell them: "I have to stop for a minute, I need to stretch. You can watch if you want."
4. Stretch naked: bend down with your legs straight, touching the ground. Then spread your legs wide. At the end, stretch out your hamstrings by sitting cross-legged.
5. When the cramp is gone, continue where you left off.

Expert's opinion

If you are going out to bonk in public, wear some wind-resistant undergarments. Yes, it will make some noise while you are at it, but at least you'll be protected from cold winds and thus prevent cramping. I know that for winter you can find double-layered models with wool and Goretex.

Testimonial

I didn't tell Christina that I had cramp and I put one of her socks in my mouth so she wouldn't hear me screaming. She must have thought I had some sort of weird dirty sock fetish...
Simon, 29

The situation

While you are shagging you are inspired to make an 18-rated film and discreetly start filming the action to capture the moment. Your partner catches you doing it.

The solution: The iKama Sutra

1. Say: "Don't take it badly; I'm not trying to make a video that I will show my colleagues tomorrow morning."
2. Add: "You know that I download apps all the time, right? Well, I have the iKama Sutra 3000 on my phone. Using the camera the phone recognizes the position I'm in and tells me what it is."
3. Point to the screen: "Here, for example, it told me we are doing it doggy style."
4. And at the end say: "There's another function: if I attach the phone to my waist, the integrated accelerometer will count the number of thrusts. It will give me a graphic and a comparison chart for the last ten days."

Expert's opinion

Nowadays, with all these phones with integrated cameras, everybody thinks they can make a good 18-cert film. In the good old days of hairy porn, nobody would imagine that the director could act, do the lighting and film at the same time...

Testimonial

I just got a brand new smartphone. When I tried filming us, I accidentally sent the live stream to all my contacts. It was my work phone...
Samantha, 25

The situation

You would like to bonk, but she is nervous and can't get excited.
You can't do it.

The solution: Doctor Dickson

1. Go with her to the nearest pharmacy.
2. Say hello to the pharmacist.
3. Tell her: "We just tried to bonk behind your trash cans. But I don't know what's wrong with her – she just can't get wet. Do you have a strong and efficient lubricant that you could recommend?"
4. Buy the lubricant she recommends (she will no doubt suggest Extreme Outdoor Bonk Oil by Dr. Dickson).
4. Apply the lubricant (leave the pharmacy first).
5. Bonk behind the trash cans.

Expert's opinion

Back in the days of hairy porn we ordered tobacco-scented lubricant wholesale straight from the factory. They shipped it to us in ten-litre buckets. Three days later we had to order more.

Testimonial

As soon as the problem arose, I knew we needed lube. I went to the fast food restaurant nearby and ordered their greasiest burger. When I came out I put my tool in the burger to grease it.
Damian, 40

The situation

You are visiting a church when you are both suddenly taken with the desire to bonk. You think that you are alone and start frolicking. Three minutes later a priest finds you shagging in the confessional.

The solution: The blown candle

1. Don't panic, a priest has very vague notions of sex. He won't understand what you were doing in his confessional.
2. Tell him: "It's very hot in your church. It's so hot that we had to take our clothes off. The confessional is the coolest part of the church that we could find."
3. Add: "If I were you, I would blow out a few of these candles. They are really heating this place, you know."
4. Watch the priest as he blows out 2,500 candles one by one.
5. Get dressed and say: "Yes, it was the candles for sure; it's already cooler in here."
6. Leave the church.

Expert's opinion

Try not to go there to bonk on Sunday mornings; according to my experience there are usually a lot of people there.

Testimonial

The priest surprised me as I was dunking my bits in the holy water to bless it before the act. I was hoping that the Lord would be a bit less angry.
Peter, 23

The situation

You are in the middle of a shag in the park. She thinks she hears someone coming and panics. Result: you are stuck inside.

The solution: The Wing nut

1. Get dressed as best you can.
2. Walk together like Siamese twins to the nearest mini-market.
   A piece of advice from our expert who has already been in this situation:
   "Make sure you both walk at the same speed in order to avoid disputes that would be very inconvenient in your situation."
3. Buy a jug of olive oil.
4. Crab-walk back to the park, olive oil in hand.
5. Apply the oil generously to the trouble zone. Ideally you should try to unscrew your partner by turning them like a wing nut, using your legs as a lever.

Expert's opinion

Did you know that a contracted vagina can apply pressure of up to 8 bars, which is equivalent to the suction of a 2800W vacuum cleaner?

Testimonial

We had to call the fire department… three times. They wouldn't believe that we were naked and stuck in each other in the Disneyland puppet house, a place for 3–11 year olds.
Valerie, 29

The situation

You are making love behind a shrubbery in the park when you feel quick, warm licks on your bum. The position you are in would make it impossible for your partner to be doing that. You turn around and see a friendly Labrador.

The solution: The First Circle of Hell

1. Tell your partner: "A Labrador has just attempted a threesome; I will try to make him go away."
2. Grab a stick and throw it as far as possible.
3. Resume your back-and-forth.
4. Unfortunately, the dog will bring the stick back to you. Throw it again and resume your activity for another 20 seconds.
5. Continue with this operation until you finish the act.

Expert's opinion

Careful, if you notice that a dog has a lead, its master is not far away, hiding and probably looking at you.

Testimonial

We were bonking in a field when a pack of fox terriers found us. They started to bark like crazy and soon six hunters arrived. We ran away as fast as deer.
Carl, 50

The situation

You are bonking in the cinema and trying to be as discreet as possible so that nobody will notice. But there is a problem: you are a damn good shag and your partner is groaning louder and louder.

The solution: The Magic Corn

1. Continue to bonk and take a big handful of popcorn.
2. Put it in your mouth and chew loudly; this should cover up the noise of your partner.
3. If that doesn't do it, put the bucket of popcorn over the head of your partner (popped corn is a very efficient soundproofing material).
4. Continue to shag while preventing your partner from taking off the popcorn helmet.

Expert's opinion

I had some doubts about this technique and I therefore tested it in the field with a sound engineer. When we analysed the audiogram of my shag, we established that with the popcorn helmet there was indeed an 11dB drop in the sound my partner was emitting.

Testimonial

We were both getting loud so we both put popcorn buckets on our heads. The problem was that because of that we couldn't see that the film finished and we were still shagging when the lights came on...
Alex and Cindy, 33

PART 4:

Many believe that once the deed is done, the mission has been accomplished. Wrong! A successful public bonk also means getting out safely, which can be just as perilous as the act itself.

PROBLEMS AFTER

What do you do when a condom gets stuck in your zip and gives you away?
How do you deal with a heartless partner who leaves you
naked in the street, attached to a street lamp?
What do you do when you mistakenly send a sexy text to your mum?

In the following pages you will discover that your life is not over
if a photo of you shagging is displayed on a giant screen
in front of 100 people, and many other potentially problematic situations.

The situation

You bonked in public. A few hours later you send your partner a text that goes something like this: "I have never been blown like that before. I love your ass and your big boobs." Once you press Send, you realize in horror that you mistakenly sent it to your mother.

The solution: The Protocol Technique

1. Don't call your mother to say: "Mother, I'm sorry for the text with bad words that I sent you."
2. Don't panic. Your mother will be too bothered about the text to bring it up. She will never mention it and she'll pretend she never got it.
3. Continue, therefore, to go to your parents for Sunday roasts and pretend nothing has happened. But be realistic, there will be three or four family dinners when the silences will seem very long.
4. During these meals, be careful not to blush when certain phrases come up, for example: "Do you want more sausage?" or "Do you want to stuff the turkey?" or "You can lick your plate."
5. And next time, double check the recipient of the texts you are sending.

Expert's opinion

My mother doesn't know how to use her phone very well. When she receives a text she always asks for help. Since I know that her friends will be reading her texts, I keep sending her anonymous sexy messages from a certain Robert.

Testimonial

I always send messages from a hidden number. My mother answered my text with one that started: "I like licking your big cock too..." I couldn't read the rest, and I definitely couldn't bring myself to open the attached image.
Tony, 22

The situation

You bonked in a rollercoaster. At the end of the ride you are proud of your achievement but are brought back to Earth when you discover a photo was taken. A very explicit photo of you is displayed at the photo stand.

The solution: The African Escape

1. Leave the area immediately (even if you really want that photo, don't buy it — you will be too embarrassed while they are printing it out).
2. Run to the nearest souvenir shop.
3. Buy a giraffe outfit (full costume for two: you will be the giraffe's front legs and your partner the back legs).
4. Remain in disguise for the rest of the day — that way security won't find you. Pretend nothing happened: have an ice cream, queue for the 3D simulator and the boat to see the little dolls singing "It's a small world…"
5. Only take off your outfit when you get to your car.

Expert's opinion

According to a poll done by a famous American amusement park, 9% of visitors associate being strapped to the leather seat of a rollercoaster with being beaten during an S&M act.

Testimonial

I caught two grannies at the photo stand. One was buying our photo in an XXXL format; the other bought a mug with it on.
Catherine, 21

You are interrupted and
your condom gets stuck in your zip

The situation

You narrowly escape being seen by a friend and pull your trousers up quickly, as if nothing had happened. But you were too fast: the condom is stuck in your zip. And it is visible!

The solution: The Twisted Giraffe

1. Tell your friend: "No, silly, this isn't a condom, it's a balloon that is simply caught in my zip."
2. Open the zip and take out the 'balloon'.
3. Blow it up with your mouth.
4. Twist it in different areas to make a cute dog or a nice giraffe.
5. Give it to your friend and tell him he can give it to his kids.

Expert's opinion

You can find fluorescent condoms that glow in the dark. Even if you find this amusing, don't play *Star Wars* with your tool; it's not a light sabre!

Testimonial

It wasn't only the condom that got stuck in the zip. I was in a lot of pain.
Paul, 30

You are photographed by an online mapping camera while bonking in your garden

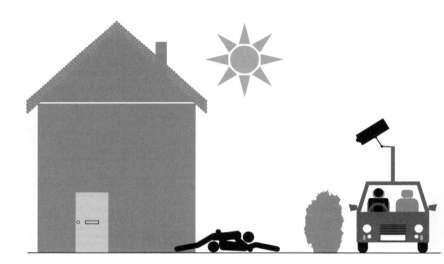

The situation:

You decide to bonk in your garden. You are very naked and very busy when you notice a vehicle equipped with cameras taking pictures of your street. The horror: a photo of you bonking is about to be put online for the world to see.

The solution: Buzz of the Century

1. Wait for your photo to appear on the internet and download it.
2. Without saying that you are its star, publish the photo on all the forums that you can find (IT forums, recipe forums, art image forums and so on). In other words, your photo should be as visible as possible; it has to be the buzz of the year.
3. Contact the mapping company and tell them about your problem: a photo of you bonking in your garden was taken by their car. Explain that it has been published on all the forums online. Make them understand that you are outraged and that you will ask for damages for the suffering this has caused you.
4. Threaten them with a lawsuit for "lack of respect for one's private life, illegal distribution of offensive images and lack of respect for your physical integrity."
5. Try to settle for 2,000,000 dollars.

Expert's opinion

I suggested to an online mapping company that they develop "Streetbonk", an application that would allow people to find the best spots for outdoor bonking. They decided to develop an art app instead. Considering the word 'sex' is the most searched on search engines, I don't understand how they don't see that people are obviously not interested in museums.

Testimonial

A neighbour must have recognized my garden on a forum because three days later there was a piece of paper over our street sign renaming it "Bonk Street". Personally I preferred "Roosevelt Street" …
Terrence, 42

The situation

You just did it in a park. When getting dressed, your buttocks start itching really badly. They are swollen and bright red — you have a grass allergy. It gets so bad that you can't pull your trousers all the way up.

The solution: Magic Powder

1. Grab a fistful of soil.
2. Put it in your underpants (yes, really).
3. Pull up your stuffed pants.
4. The soil is rich in healing substances and the contact will calm your itch.
5. Go home and try walking normally. If someone sees you walking oddly, they will think that you pooped your pants — and the soil you are carrying won't help persuade them otherwise.
6. When you get to a pharmacy, ask for the strongest antihistamine they have. Reminder: antihistamine pills are always taken orally, not... locally.

Expert's opinion

Or you can go home wearing your trousers below your buttocks, baggy-style. Baggy style actually came from cheap porn: by having actors keep their pants half off between scenes, they saved precious seconds of production time.

Testimonial

What irritated my skin were the fire ants on which I had the misfortune to sit. It burned for days!
Julian, 32

You are stuck in the middle of the street with pink handcuffs

The situation:

Your partner wanted to spice up your public bonk by cuffing you to a lamp post with pink furry handcuffs. They left with the keys – and left you half naked in a public area. You can't even reach down and pull up your trousers.

The solution: The Penguin Technique

1. Evaluate the situation: people will be frightened to see you handcuffed and with your trousers round your ankles. If you ask them to help you pull up your pants, they will run in horror.
2. Walking like a penguin, go towards the passers-by and tell them: "No, don't leave. I am not a dangerous pervert. And no, I didn't escape from Pink Prison."
3. Add: "I will pay £100 to whoever pulls up my trousers!"
4. Don't lose hope: 1 person in 600 will say yes.
5. Once your trousers are up, tell the person who helped you to take the money out of your wallet in your pocket. (If you don't have it, run.)
6. Go home.

Expert's opinion

My neighbour bonks in public all the time, but his girlfriend sometimes plays bad tricks on him. Last week he called me because he was handcuffed half-naked to a supermarket trolley.

Testimonial

I found myself attached to a lamppost in the middle of the street. Slowly around 50 passers-by gathered around me. They thought I was a magician and that I was going to perform an impressive escape. Sadly for them, the show never happened.
Alex, 33

PART 5:

Before attempting to bonk outdoors, some of you will take
some time to train and go through the theory.
Others need a warm-up before.

PROBLEMS DURING TRAINING AND WARM-UP

Which equipment do you need and how do you get it ready? What will you do if you are caught with a huge sex toy at the bank? How do you keep your dignity when a family friend sees you leaving a sex shop with an inflatable doll?

In the following pages you will find out that it is possible to pick up a good porn DVD at the dispenser without being caught by your mother who just happens to be walking past at that same moment.

You are caught measuring your tool

The situation

You are in a big furniture Swedish furniture shop. As always you picked up the paper measuring tape at the entrance. An hour later you can't fight your curiosity and decide to use it to finally find out the size of your tool. No luck: you are caught behind the HJORGE KJOK closet in full... measure.

The solution: The Frösüt Technique

1. Let's face it, you are in trouble.
2. Don't pull your trousers up and tell the shop assistant: "This is not what it looks like. When I was measuring your FRÖSÜT chair, I realized that your tape measures were not properly calibrated."
3. Don't let the shop assistant interrupt you.
4. Continue firmly: "I know my penis length exactly: it is 28.32cm. Look, your measure says it is less than 6.4 cm. That's impossible."
5. Don't wait for the assistant's answer, they won't give you one.
6. Drop the candles, plastic bottles and paper napkins and leave as quickly as possible.

Expert's opinion

In case you didn't know, Ikea's paper tool is perfect for such measuring. It lets you find out not only the length, but also the circumference of your tool, free of charge. Using the simple cylinder formula you can also calculate the volume.

Testimonial

Another client interrupted us and suggested he check my claim by measuring his tool too. The assistant left before he could even finish his sentence.
Philip, 25

The situation

You are at the bank and you put your phone on vibrate. During the meeting with your banker, the phone starts vibrating in your bag. You grab the wrong thing in your bag and you take out a big steel vibrator that is buzzing madly.

The solution: The Big Cylinder

1. Don't panic and don't try to camouflage your vibrator. Your banker saw it.
2. Press "Off" to make it stop vibrating.
3. Bring it to your ear and say: "Hello?"
4. Pretend to have a brief conversation.
5. When you hang up, tell your banker: "I'm sorry to have to say this, but you are looking at me with a bit of a quizzical look. Have you never seen a big, pink, battery-operated telephone?"

Expert's opinion

When I was in China I saw a ten-in-one cylindrical phone. I remember it played mp3s, had an Internet connection, a camera, and could be used as a pastry roller, a torch, a thermos, a vibrator and some other things. I'm not sure it was legal outside China...

Testimonial

As soon as he saw the sex toy, my banker said: "Oh yes Miriam, dominate me and spank me with my mouse, right here on the desk!" I left and, as I turned around, he was licking his mouse and looking at me suggestively, trying to make me stay.
Miriam, 36

110

The situation

You decide to pick up a porn DVD from a dispenser. No luck: just as you validate your choice on the screen, you mother appears behind you.

The solution: The Branko del Bonko

1. As soon as your mother starts talking to you, say: "Madam, please stop, we don't know each other."
2. As she gasps, tell her loudly and clearly so that everyone in the queue can hear you: "Will you please leave me alone? I will not help you choose the best *Branko Del Bonko* porn DVD!"
3. Leave and go watch your DVD (hopefully you don't live with your mother).
4. Look surprised when your mother tells you the story of your double that she saw at the local Blockbuster.

Expert's opinion

I am saddened by the widespread rental of 18-rated films. Back in my time, the films were only shown in cinemas. There was always debate in the cinema café afterwards so that the story, the set, the costumes, the dialogue and of course the featured new positions could be discussed.

Testimonial

I took my dad's credit card. As I selected the film, the machine indicated: "DVD already rented seven times. Are you sure you want to rent the film *The Nurse With No Panties 6*? for the 8th time?
Dennis, 19

The situation

Hoping for an outdoor bonk during the day, you go to work in a skirt and decide not to wear your knickers. Later that day you have dinner with friends and one of them points this out loudly.

The solution: The Natural Ventilator

1. Say: "Dennis, of course I have no knickers on; it's Tuesday! Every Tuesday I ventilate, as *Cosmo* advises."
2. Add: "Since I've been doing it I've cured my yeast infection and I haven't had any itching. That uncomfortable intimate itch? Gone!"
3. Turn toward your girlfriend and tell her: "You should do it too, I'm sure it will help with the redness you've been noticing."
4. Finish by saying: "And as for you, Dennis, your tool could use a bit of ventilation too. Your flute is starting to mould."
5. Ask if anyone wants more salad. They will probably answer "no".

Expert's opinion

I have always had a careful beauty routine for my penis: deep cleansing, exfoliation, clay mask, anti-wrinkle cream. I also wet-gel my pubic hair.

Testimonial

My girlfriend wanted to bonk outside. She put on knickers with a strategically placed hole. Since it was quite cold she also put on her tights. Sometimes she can be really dumb… *Mathias, 32*

The situation

Since you haven't been having sex in public, you go to a sex shop to buy an outdoor bonk DVD. As luck would have it, you are seen coming out by your parents' best friend; and he recognizes you.

The solution: The Vengeful Justice Upholder

1. Switch from "I'm sneaking out of a sex shop hoping not to be seen" mode to a confident and firm attitude.
2. Yell into his face: "You are still loitering around the sex shop? Don't you have anything better to do?"
3. He will tell you that it's you who is leaving the sex shop.
4. Tell him: "Stop lying, I just talked to the store manager and he told me that you bought the *Mega Bonk at Seaworld* DVD yesterday. I bought it so I could show my parents what kind of films you like to watch."
5. Leave while saying to him that you are doing this to help him get out of the sex inferno he has found himself in.

Expert's opinion

An online sex shop didn't find it necessary to camouflage its shipments. Its clients were having some embarrassing moments when picking up their deliveries at the local post office... The boxes were clearly labelled with the name of the shop, The Mega Porn Emporium, with a big photo of the products that they ordered.

Testimonial

The sex shop I went to was closing, so most of their products were on sale at 70% off. I went for it and bought 75 DVDs at £1 each. As I was loading up the boot of my car I found myself face to face with my boss. He had gone for a stroll around the neighbourhood.
Eric, 45

PART 6:

Do you have a passion for DIY projects
and are proud of yourself for it?

How to make organic, fair trade sex toys

You can't bear the fact that your sex toys
were made by children in China or Cambodia?

You refuse to eat or lick anything that isn't organic?

Find out in the following pages how an ordinary belt and
an orange can spice up a bonk session in the park!

How to make organic fishnet stockings

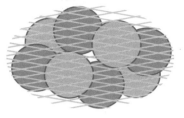

1. Buy 3 kg of the cheapest oranges in a mesh bag.

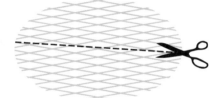

2. Cut the mesh lengthwise.

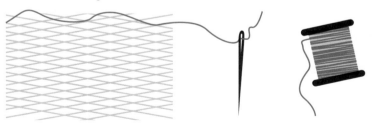

3. Use thread or an electric cable (use what you find nearest) to sew nice stockings. Slip on the stockings. Tip: if you end up with leftover mesh, use it to make some stylish gloves.

How to make an organic ball gag

1. Buy an organic tangerine at the nearest organic store.

2. Pierce it through to make a wide incision.

3. Slide your belt through the fruit.

Place the gag into your mouth, all the while appreciating the lovely taste of the tangerine. Bite into it if you are thirsty while making the effort, or if you feel you need some vitamins.

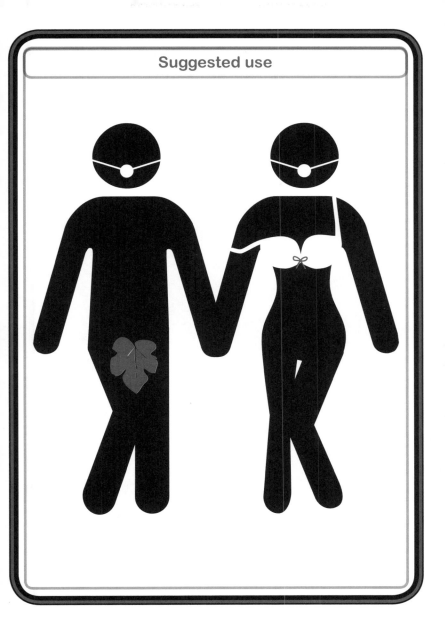

121

How to make a refreshing organic lubricant

1. Buy 2l of basic olive oil

2. Buy 1l of cheap mint syrup.

3. Add the surprise ingredient (don't tell your partner what it is).

4. Mix all of the olive oil, mint syrup and chicken sauce
in a champagne bucket (just because it's organic it doesn't
have to be cheap!). Mix vigorously for five minutes with your hands. Done!

How to make an organic whip

1. Buy an organic leek in the nearest organic supermarket.

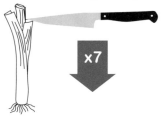

2. Cut it seven times from top to bottom (those who prefer a kinkier whip can try more creative cuts).

3. Your whip is ready to be used. Please note: even if you are very hungry, do not eat your raw leek whip. Not only will you be short of a toy, you will also have a heinous breath.

How to make a gimp mask with birthday balloons

1. Buy a balloon.

2. Cut the balloon at its base with scissors.

3. Cut a hole for the eyes.

4. Cut a hole for the nose.

5. Cut a hole for your mouth (without it you will quickly suffocate).

Suggested use

How to make an organic artificial vagina

1. Buy a portion of Asian noodles at the nearest Chinese restaurant
   (tip: ask for non-spicy ones!).

2. Buy a plastic bottle with a wide rim.

3. Put the noodles in the bottle
   (make sure to cool them down to about
   37°C; anything above that would be painful).

How to make an inflatable blow-up doll that can also be used in the sea or at the beach

1. Buy an inflatable crocodile.

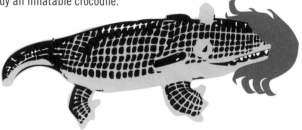

2. Put some green algae on its head (as if the crocodile had a green wig).

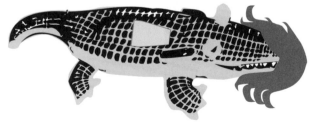

3. Glue the artificial vagina (*see above*) on the back of the crocodile. Be careful: the access hole should be oriented towards the back, otherwise you will be 69-ing the crocodile).

PART 7:

The time has come for you to see if you have understood well the philosophy and the power of the tips we have given you in this book.